# Poetry Behind the Walls

# Jyjuan Brock

Behind the Walls written by Jyjuan Brock

Published by Writers Block Publishing LLC

www.writersblockpublishingllc.com

For more information about Jyjuan Brock contact Angela Brock at angelabrock82@yahoo.com

# Poetry Behind the Walls

## Acknowledgement

First I would like to thank God for the gift of writing.
Rev. Marcus Harvey for being there as my mentor.

Heinz Endowment: Carmen Anderson and Vicki Beattiefor hearing my voice and gave me the motivation to write.

Special thanks to the ladies who supported my mom
Special thanks to my lawyers

Federal Attorney Jay Finkelstein and Attorney Kevin Trower and last the woman of my life, my mother who gave me the strength and courage through all this.

# Jyjuan Brock

## A Mother's Love

It takes a strong determined woman
to carry another life inside one of life's most precious gifts,
that bond; the two eternally for a lifetime.
the pain endured to birth a child
Only a mother knows

She's built to stand the test of time,
yet as delicate as a rose.
A mother love is an emotion
that shines brighter than the sun.

She'll bandage bumps and bruises if you're hurt,
and is always there to cheer you on.
She will sacrifice and whether wrong or right,
always willing to put up a fight during the
darkest days and coldest nights, but what's wrong is wrong
and what right is right.

A mother is a woman that can birth and raise a child
Who ever knew that she could love some one
more than life allows?

That's why her bond is twice as strong,
she is no ending to her chapters love, embrace,
and a smiling face is the only thing that matters.
Like a lioness, she protects her cubs
with everything she has.
And sometime plays a double role with the
absence of a dad.
I appreciate you everyday
For all you persevered

# Poetry Behind the Walls

That love is unconditional
Through all the moments that we shared.

# Jyjuan Brock

## The Pain is Real

The way I was living wasn't living.
Head barely above water
Still hung in the same crowds,
still dealt with the same circles
So it was easy come easy go.

 Anything worth living for was
always etched out in a block of stone.
The way life was headed
I would of end up dead or all alone
There's always a story to tell
Staring through millions of cold dark eyes
But deep down there are more than a million lies.

We try to hide and disguise from the millions of other
Prying and deceiving eyes
They are indeed the mirror of the soul
Some eyes are young and some of them are old
You just need to know which road to follow
while some are straight and cluttered.
The other are old and hollow
I was told to be a leader and never one to follow

As I sit in my space, I've realized I wasted so much
potential and time with so much at stake.
Never realizing what was really on the line.
Living for the wrong reason different women for
different seasons and each served as a specific lesson
Some I thought was love

# Poetry Behind the Walls

In reality they were stressors

But in the end, there was no real meaning
It was never about love just distrust and misleading,
or maybe I was yearning for that personal feeling
thinking like Marvin when he wrote *Sexual Healing*
Almost like a drug now my body is going through
withdrawn and I'm feeling all alone.

A house is just a house and a home is just a home
You have to build your own foundation
so you can make it your own.
To say my pain is real is a true understatement
I see it through the tears in my eyes and the cracks in the
pavement.
All this time and talent wasted, so strong I just can't
shake it.
But I have to stand tall like a man
Head held high and face this the pain is real!

# Jyjuan Brock

## Hurt Beyond Repair

Sometimes a person's love could be misunderstood,
and time is a friend to all that is good.
Patience is a virtue and you'll need that too.
Why can't I take back the love that I've given to you?

I wish you could feel all this hurt; all the pain.
The loyalty is gone so it will never be the same.
At one point, I thought above sharing my last name
Rain poured out my tears, but the hurt still remains

Certain things in life they just wouldn't understand
Being taken for granted wasn't the part of the plan
At times I wish I could replace you
Make my heart turn cold and convince myself to hate you

Teaching a person to love was my form of motivation,
but how can you love someone whom doesn't know what
love is? It's like swimming without water
 or walking across a burnt bridge.

Now I'm all alone my hearts pounding in your absence
But I can't keep living in the past, keep moving towards
the present.
Time waits for no man, so make every moments
precious, and everyone's not worth your love.
So be cautious how you spend it
Because true love has no boundaries, stipulation, or
limits.

# Poetry Behind the Walls

## Devil in Disguise

He was once an angel, true intention tried to hide.
Always smiling in your face, but their eyes tell a different
side.

Could never see the wrong they've done,
someone else was always the blame.
The devil comes in many forms, although intentions
never change.
They point out all the bad you've done
but never the good.
When you point out fuck up shit they do
they claim, it's because of you!!!

Never an apology.
To them they're always right.
My body screamed deep down inside
"The devil is a lie!"
Praying on your demise and praying for you to fall.
Just to throw it in your face, and scream what you did
wrong.

So instead of speaking what I feel, my feelings I always
hide because there no point of arguing with the devil in
disguise.

# Jyjuan Brock

## My Sacred Vowels

My words cannot explain the way you make me feel.
You've bandage all my wounds in time they will heal.
You were there as my crutch when I fell down and
broken when I needed time to vent.

Your ears were always open so you became the one!
The woman I have chosen through all our ups and downs.
I swear to God you'll never lose me as long as you play
your part.

Through good and bad, rich are poor.
Through rain or sun we can be the power couple.
Envied by all the others

It's always best when you could be best friends as well as
lovers. In time we both will really know who's really
down for one another?

So you can give me all of you and tell me all your secrets
I will never tell a soul.
In my heart is where I'll keep them.
These are my secret vowels for you it remain the same.
All I ask in return is for you never change

So I ask God for forgiveness, and I'm asking you the
same. For all the sins I've ever done and all the mistakes
that I made.

My Sacred Vowels!!

# Poetry Behind the Walls

## Wiseman Tell

My O.G. taught me never to be delusional.

Constantly keep a poker face play; the hand that life has given you.

History repeats itself only with different people.
Same group you thought were friends were the same people using you; embarrassing you.
Fake tears mourning at your funeral.

Keep the grass cut.
Always staring through your peripheral.
Snakes smiling in your face.
Intentions were to bury you.
Tha game that he was spitting.

Opened my eyes up to the bitter truth.
Don't dwell too much on the past.
Focus on what's in front of you
Shot's fired
Man down
Battle scars turn into bullet wounds

Everybody bleeds the same and anybody is bullet proof.
I should have listen to my old head and all the things he told me not to do.
Knowledge is power.
Proper guidance allows room to improve.
Stay humble, move silent.

# Jyjuan Brock

Calculate your every move.
Keep under the radar.
Anticipate to take a loss or two.
Learn how to move; how bosses move.

Secure the bag and count that cash until your fingerprints
are black and blue.
If a persons' eating off your plate.
Make sure they order extra food.
Nothing in life is ever free.
Always remember the Golden Rule.
When you're sitting at the table, keep your mouth closed
when you're eating food.

Get snakes and rats out of your kitchen so you could get
until your bellies full.
Become a wolf in sheep's clothing where survival is the
only rule.

This game isn't for everyone.
Use caution on the lane you choose.
Just because a person is close in age doesn't make them
equal.

Never get emotional, it's business, never personal

# Poetry Behind the Walls

## Friends, How Many Of Us Have Them

Not enough friends, far too many enemies
with so much that come from those whom pretend to be.
Some are distant relatives, while others are no kin to me.
But what more can you ask for when closest friends
become your enemies.

Through all the lies and deception
I use my mind as a weapon
To decipher all the anger
All the hate and aggression
A hard head makes a soft ass
I took that as a lesson
Like when a person shows their true colors
take heed and consider that a blessing

Now the eyes will tell the tale of a person's insecurities
sparks a flame full of hurt, and animosity when attentions
shine through a person soul and show their
transparencies.
This is the type of shit make me start to hate love

I ask myself, time and time again what type of person
really fake love unless there attentions weren't never
really pure, and they showed you what they are made of.
That's when you have to tell yourself
Decisions must be made up
It not like you really gave up

## Jyjuan Brock

But what choices have they gave us?
You have to do what's best for self, when things didn't
seem to add up.
Sometimes the warning signs are there.
It's by choice for you to listen.
When a person's smile turns upside down
How many choices must be given?

# Poetry Behind the Walls

## Action Speak Louder Than Words

Don't sleep when I tell you the way that I felt
About the life that I lived
Or the hand that was dealt.

With my feet to the ground, and my ear to the street
Time waits for no one
So always think before you speak.

Because actions have a way
Of speaking louder than words
Always speak on how you feel,
and demand what you deserve

Closed mouths don't get fed
That's what I was always told
Start from the beginning to the end
and from the new to the old

With my mind made up
That things are destined to change
You might see what I see
But our visions not the same

# Jyjuan Brock

## Over THE DEEP END

Total isolation, out of sight out of mind.
Days and nights are never promised always, always keep
the faith alive.

Generational gap where we still struggle to survive.
Corrupted to a system where snitching is at a- all- time
high.

Those of us that didn't make it, keep their memory alive.
The seconds keep ticking as we're running out of time.
No time for doubt when your life is on the line.
We're always being watch even if we're first to die.

Alone in a cell thinking of better ways to survive.
Situation lying dormant thoughts racing through my mind
It like *damn.*

Shit got me toss and turning in my sleep.
An outer body experience that's far from just a normal
dream.
Self-expression that I saw was a reflection of
authenticity.

Once reality has set in, my superstition intervened.
I finally understood why they would never understand
me.
Once a person can't touch who you've become, they'll dig
up what you used to be.

# Poetry Behind the Walls

Only scratching the surface, most wounds are more than
skin deep.
While the enemy of an enemy becomes closer than your
family, their motives may be different, but both share a
common link.

By looking in the mirror, I saw a reflection staring right
back at me.
If I committed a crime, no one could do the time but me.
Closest friend become distant, anger brewing from
animosity.
Although it took some time, I had to respect how other
people think.

Confession of why I never seemed to learn my lesson
By being loyal to a fault was a curse that I accepted.
The stress and aggression kept me from placing second.
Wishing I would have listened to more than intuition
Saving self from the pain of knowing the true meaning of
friendship.

Circle continued to shrink; still I look it as a blessing
Couldn't get any addresses, phone numbers was none
listed.
Sometimes I sit and wonder did I ever really miss them.
Or if my circumstances were a divine intervention
Never knew how it would feel corrupting the minds of
our children.

# Jyjuan Brock

Might not be their true intention, that's why people only play there lane that life intended.
Realization kicking in now in coming to my senses of how it feels left without a dollar or a visit.

No one can grasp the concept if they have never had to live it.
The pain inside can burn down the walls of every jail and every prison.
Hiding in plain sight, trying not to be transparent.
Once a person spots your flaws, they'll utilize it as a weakness.

It isn't justice designed to break down our spirit
Living so close to death can lead to dire consequences.
If the laws never change in the streets and the prisons.
If I abided by the law would my life have turned out differently? With a monkey on our back and a pain that's self-inflicted by challenging a man's pride, his morals, and integrity.

This isn't jail, it's just another version of slavery where they trade us off as stock, another face turned into memory.
How is it possible to change if we never built up our legacy?
In a world designed to snatch your innocence over mistaken identity.
Instead of resources for reform, they'll build more penitentiaries.

# Poetry Behind the Walls

Knowing the society never intended for justice or mutual equality.
So how is it really justice if we never treated equally?
This is the reason for all the anger, aggression, and hostility.

Racism never died, it just goes by a different name.
The courts claims to be indifferent although the laws will never change.
Cards of life come falling down because the odds are stacked against us.

Pressure burst pipes as I struggle just to finish.
Every limit beyond normal recognition.
To them where like the crabs inside a barrel, and everybody wants to be the victor.
Making over the deep end, is the only way to save us
Our parents always told us that we were destined for greatness.

# Jyjuan Brock

## Child Abuse

There are a few things in my past no kid should ever
have to go through.
Snatching a child innocence is both unusual and cruel.
Used to scare us half to death or hang us off the roof
Beaten within an inch of life, mother suffered the same
abuse.

He heard the screams and the cries stop; still he hit us
even more.
I use to play a game to block the pain, in the end there
was no use.
If I didn't cry, he would apply more force in his follow
through.
My mom tried to protect me and my brother too
She again became a victim of the pain of his abuse

I wonder how he would felt to be placed inside our shoes
So he could feel every inch of pain he made us go
through.
He beat us like we stole his check. He felt he had a point
to prove.
He made us cover up our bruises, to hide the truth

At the time I didn't understand, the reasons for his moods
Some days I would hide and wait afraid to go to school
Coached me on what not to say, it wasn't the honest thing
to do.
He blamed it on the crack cocaine, but that's not a good
excuse.

# Poetry Behind the Walls

That man was high off more than weed and had nothing to lose.
Was a carpenter by day, so his hands he always used
How can you beat a mom and child that once claimed to love?
If I could end his life today for all the pain throughout the years, I would gladly put my handcuffs on, and walk myself to jail.

# Jyjuan Brock

## The Breakdown

When I wasn't living right, my circumstances had to change.
Reality began to show signs, or how weak I have became
No longer using common sense any thinking was impaired.

Trying to focus too much on my past when my futures straight ahead.
Instead of playing chess, greed took over my head.
Gossip will get you caught up, with distortions of the truth.
Eye are watching everywhere searching for pattern in how you move.

Coming from an era where loyalty isn't the same.
Best friends will sell you out for a little financial gain.
As we grow older, people and priorities tend to change
Damn, near brothers grow up, until money got in the way.

It's a shame that a little change,
could lead to shots being exchanged.
Jealousy breeds envy which helped ignite the flame
When its business, never let feelings or emotions get in the way.
Greed will keep an advisory loyal as long as you continue to feed them.
In the eyes of the public, those people are labeled leeches

# Poetry Behind the Walls

Once they got all that they can get, you'll see a change in their demeanor.

Next to women, money will forever be the route of evil. Just because they make a little money, that doesn't make them your equal.

Grinding without a plan is like having nothing to lose.
Never count what's in another man's pockets, focus on what you have to do.
You have to show self-confidence, tho' you have nothing to prove.
If you don't believe in yourself, why would someone else believe in you?

# Jyjuan Brock

## Fantasy

How can a person provoke hate
if the never felt what love is?

One of life's strongest emotions
Impairing our judgements
Don't get caught in the moment

Thoughts got her wide open.
Faint scents of wild roses
keep pulling her closer
Dim lighting from candles
Rose pedals, and bubbles
The taste of champagne
As she slowly bends over

The warmth of his touch
while massaging her shoulders
Soft kisses all over
It's too soon to be over

Mind started racing
Her heart start to flutter
The flower just blossomed
Exposing its color
Her dam starts to burst
Walls starting to crumble

# Poetry Behind the Walls

## Finding the Write One

We search the world both far and wide for the partner of
our dreams
One that fills the empty void and makes our life complete

Life's purpose is creating memories that's both intriguing
and unique.
With moments that take our breath away and knocks us
off our feet.

Many will walk into our lives, that doesn't mean they're
meant to be.
Special ones leave foot prints in the sand for a lasting
memory.

In the eye of the beholder, beauty is more than surface
deep
Relationships are built off compromise and compatibility
In the pursuit of happiness, fate insures that one day we
will meet.

We may be laying with a beauty, but inside were dealing
with a beast.
A sophisticated mind; personality just as sweet
A look of total innocence, but a freak between the sheets
One that is book smart, with common knowledge of the
streets.

# Jyjuan Brock

No need to knock on any door I already have the key
but until that day we turn our dreams into reality
always keep you heart pure and save a space that's just
for me.

Together forever and a day building endless memories.
Every quality that you could ever want and all the love
you'll ever need.

True love can conquer all, but respect is everything
When two unite as one, hearts instantly sync.
With a heart that's made of solid gold, compassion, and
empathy, what more could be asked for, if two souls are
meant to be.

That's why a calm mind makes rational decisions
There is more to life than living with regret and
consequences.
Once tie is invested, and the hearts are fully committed
by first becoming friends and respecting each other's
wishes heart beat racing, soft touches, light kisses.

Whenever in their presence an indescribable weakness,
butterflies in my stomach, the feeling of motion sickness.
The brain is sending mixed signals, but my body is
saying something different.

Intimate positions, while making adult decisions
Exploring each other's secret, what's our strength, what's
our weakness?

# Poetry Behind the Walls

Don't ever take for granted affection when it is given.
It's hard enough to find true love the way that God
intended.

With no hidden agendas, secret motives, or incentives
but one that is pure, one hundred percent authentic.
Learning Other's Values and Emotion, our journey has
been completed.

## Jyjuan Brock

## True Love Is Hard To Find

For every grain of jet black sand
inside my hour glass
as days turn into longer nights,
and years begin to pass
over shadowed by distorted thoughts.
From the downpours I've endured
You've showed me there were better days.

At the end of every storm
through the clouds
though well endowed
still had to carry on
mind was searching for a rainbow
because you were my pot of gold
Both hearts drum to a familiar beat, and unite the two as
one.

Positive perception
is like a rose without its thorns.
By conquering your heart
you've introduced me to your world.

# Poetry Behind the Walls

Stimulated by more than just your mind
True connection through our souls
I appreciate you everyday
For all that you have done
You are so opinionated
And always speaks what's on your mind
we're connected in more ways than one
True love is hard to find!!!

# Jyjuan Brock

## A House is Just a House No One Wants to Be Alone

Filled with happiness and laughter
Leaving the past in the past
Focusing on what really matters
In hopes that following my heart
Doesn't lead me to diaster

There is so many questions
That I would really like to ask her
Like what's your future goals, favorite foods, and
favorite actors

Trying my best to fill a void
And see what I'm really after
Sometimes it's a lot more than meets the eye

When certain questions unfold
The eyes will tell a million tales
They're the mirror of the soul.
Who am I judge
About a person's past
We all have a story.

Behind the struggles that we've had
All I can do is pray
That you are nothing like my last
as the days turn nights.

# Poetry Behind the Walls

And years proceed to pass
Became a personal obsession
Emotions grew far beyond our hearts

And we cherished every second
You came to me from up above
I consider that a blessing
We'll never let each other go
Because there's too time invested

At the end of the day
No one wants to be alone
A house is just a house
Until we make it into home

# Jyjuan Brock

## In My Thoughts

Are you living or existing?
The two are differently defined
Understanding that there will always be a reaction
For every action in my life

One thing that we could never get back
Is all the time the clock rewinds.
Nine-Tenths of all wisdom
Consists of being wise in time.

Once the clock breaks, you can no longer rely
On what the clock reads 98% of the time.
Existing is instinctual, self-preservation.
Living is survival; life is only what you make it

From an emotional stand point,
the world is mines for have been taken.
Intelligent of a genius, but mentally unstable.
If I don't accept accountability,
I'll misdiagnose every problem.
If I mistreat a diagnoses,
things will not proceed to prosper

Part of healing is self-acceptance
and understanding your homework.
To recognize that self-defeating excuses won't work.
Now confined inside a little box, understanding why I
really lost.

# Poetry Behind the Walls

It takes a man to understand, that everybody takes a loss.
What matters is how you handle it.
And if you bounce back twice as strong.
It takes a bigger man to comprehend
How hard it is to live a life you lost.

# Jyjuan Brock

## Baby Girl is a Ryder

What's understood doesn't need to be explained
was there through all the ups and downs

The darkest moments she remained
promised to never break the bond
with me she never changed.

It was never about the money
Because she understood the game
She was my golden link
That connected every chain

She stayed throughout the struggles
My best friend she has became
You can't pay for loyalty.
The streets aren't what they used to be
The eyes will tell a lie.

And show you things you weren't meant to see
that's why she was my extra set.
To show me things I didn't see
you'll never know if as person's loyal.
Until it's not easy to be
She outlasted all my niggas
All my friends
All my enemies
Along with all those fake ass bitches
That pretend to be
She is my ryder.

## Poetry Behind the Walls

For that I'm forever grateful
It's hard to find a woman
with these qualities
That is faithful

For every test I threw her way
she passed with flying colors
It's easy for me to tell the world
How much I really love her
She became my best friend
Before we were ever lovers
She rode it out through everything
Even in stormy weather
Baby girl is a Ryder

# Jyjuan Brock

## Trapped

*Trapped* in a cage like an animal in the zoo.
Caught up in an indictment for charges I didn't do.
Fed's picked it up because the state had no solid proof.
No witness, no case, but the feds play by their own set of
rules.

*Trapped* in a cell, transported to different prisons.
I wish I woulda listened instead of being hard headed.
Confined to solitary, reality starts to kick in.
Just another black life lost to the system.

*Trapped* In an addiction where hustling became my drug
of reason. That Monkey on my back because I started
getting greedy. It is hard to walk away when the money
is coming so easy. The devil in your ear while the angels
the voice of reason.

*Trapped* In a hole because I knew I wasn't thinking.
Realizing that my motives was all of the wrong reasons.
Stressing about my kids when I'm the cause of why I
couldn't see them. Praying for my higher power,
Because change is never easy.

# Poetry Behind the Walls

*Trapped* Because they were right and I choose not to
listen.  Mad cuz the one I least expected was the one that
caught me slipping. Now I'm sitting in a prison hoping a
lighter sentence. My Momma always told me my troubles
are always caused by different women. That's how I
always end up in positions that life had never attended.

*Trapped* Because my heart was stuck in the position.
Soul turned cold, absolutely no fucken given
The die has been cast, but all the numbers were missing
I couldn't figure out what I did or how I did it Now I'm
*Trapped* and I got to start over from the beginning.

## Jyjuan Brock

## Transformation of Self

Sometimes it's hard to make a personal sacrifice
Through life's trials and misdeeds,
where things aren't always right.

Most battles fought from within
never rise to the surface.
Can't always live in the moment
Your life gotta have a purpose.

Only give your love
To those people that deserve it.
Gotta stay focused.
Always know what your worth is.
If you keep looking back

You're gonna trip moving forward.
And misery loves company
Our mothers always warned us.
Let the past be the past
Always keep pushing forward
Although you cannot pay for happiness
Some still can't afford it.

# Poetry Behind the Walls

## Transformation of Self; Part Two

Certain things just weren't meant to be
In life, things aren't as they seem

The demons that we fight inside
Won't have the space to coincide

Get the proper help you need
For those battles that we try to hide.

So pay close attention to the signs that weren't mentioned
Before your happiness is compromised
And your piece of mind is missing.

Try to stay ten steps ahead
Never speak it into existence
Keep an eye out for the enemy.

Learn to use your intuition
The eyes will tell a story
Of a person's true intentions
But the only way to truly learn
Is to get it out your system
Or risk everything you ever love.

# Jyjuan Brock

## Transformation of Self, Part Three

The devil was an angel
Who could blend into many places.
He fuels that fire of desire
Even in familiar faces.

He could take on the form
Of any and everything
With promises of riches
Endless wealth and even fame

But can you tell me
What that's really worth to you are me?
When you eventually have to face the truth
And you brought back to reality

A person without honor
Dishonors everything.
How can you really be a man
if you lost your integrity?
So live and let live, and learn to let go
Some friends are full of jealousy
Don't ever sell your soul.

# Poetry Behind the Walls

## Transformation of Self Part Four

If you choose not to listen
always lead by example.
You're not the only person watching
time waits for no one.

Try to keep yourself from drowning
Damm,

Why I still feel the way I feel?
It's like my mind is driving drunk
With my thought behind the wheel
I write because it's hard to talk
About emotions that I feel
And that extra space inside your brain
Some people don't deserve it

Time can heal all wounds
That were buried beneath the surface
So don't pick at the scab
That's already fully healed
Don't ever open up a wound
That was hard to conceal

# Jyjuan Brock

## I'm Sorry
By Angela Brock

I'm sitting here editing my son's poems and started to relive the pain we both endure. Wondering if I was the blame of his pain. Mind started reminiscing and visualizing the trauma he went through and because I was in my addiction, I didn't have the ability to protect me or him.

Pain, pain go away I wish this was a dream that I can take away. Son, I'm sorry for choosing the wrong man to enter into our life. I start asking God for mercy on our life. Through opening up my old wounds I promise you this will never happen to you. Like a lioness protective over cubs, through our pain we will both gain strength, and my word to God we will get through this. If it didn't kill us all it can do is make us stronger.

Pain, pain please go away. I always told him the pen is the most powerful tool, too release any anger, resentment, fear, disappointment, failure, setback, and can healing. I'm happy to call you my son you are becoming the man God wanted you to be; with a purpose.

Remember our story gives use glory, and every test is a testimony.

# Poetry Behind the Walls

## Biography

I've often been asked, how I came up with some of my ideas when I write my poetry. I am a firm believer of speaking from the heart, and allowing my brains to compose and orchestrate a symphony of my ideas. My life experiences both inside and out of jail, created a mirror, that showed a distorted version of my life. The thought process I've imposed, tries to depict every emotion I felt during the writing process. I want my readers to feel every stitch of pain, hurt, lust, desire, and solitude my writings have to offer. I've been through a long journey and sustained a whole lot of bumps and bruises along the way. The ordeals a person goes through in life gives them character, resilience, and the power trudge through life and obstacles thrown their way, and I am no different. This journey that I had to take helped me find myself, while potentially saving my life in the process. These prison bars *do not* make me any different from the next man or woman, but my writing does. My visual interpretation allows my thoughts and words to flow freely, as if my pen were directly linked to the heart itself. It is a continuous struggle, though every day is a new learning experience with a new platform for me to create poetry. I find solace in my writings. Although I am incarcerated, I refuse to allow the prison system to corrupt my mind nor my thoughts. Writing gives me the opportunity to create a foundation where I can ultimately use my poetry as a positive form of self-expression. Lastly, it gives me a voice for my words to be heard....

# Jyjuan Brock

Now let me tell my story. How can you fight a war that you don't even know exists? How can you defeat an enemy that lives within myself? What I was once told was, what you don't know can't hurt you, and honestly it's true because knowledge is power. At the age of six my innocence was taking away from me at a blink of the eye, once was a happy kid until an abusive step-dad came into me and my mother's life. I became a product of my environment. Watching my mother being abuse and me a 6 or 7 year old child put in a position to protect her. Given our poverty stricken society, I was brought up looking for acceptance and love in all the wrong places. Drug addicted mom, father non-existent and my brother's father mentally, physically, verbally, and emotionally abuse both my mother and I due in part to crack addiction. Feeling as though nothing you ever did was good enough and maybe that was the reason for the cruel and unusual punishment. Things like this will shatter any child's self-esteem and self-worth, give a child nightmares for years to come, and make an innocent child resent the law for allowing these things to happen. So what is a kid to do with no outlet and being forced to hide feelings and emotions to society? You eventually become unstable and what most people call a product of their environment.

I had a brother, actually three brothers, who never got a chance to share their stories. They all died within the past two years, two because of gun violence and one because of drugs, and never was able to tell their story. All wars are won or lost within. I'm finally beginning to realize that it's an inside job. Now I'm dealing with the criminal justice system due to unresolved issues that haunted me majority of my life, mental health" due to the trauma I never address.

We are brought up in a society where we are separated by invisible barriers and geographical boundaries. Where the youth look up to the neighborhood drug dealers and think life is a game. But unlike PlayStation, we can't hit the reset button. We can't start over from the beginning if we die.

# Jyjuan Brock

Made in the USA
Middletown, DE
23 July 2022

69913708R00028